Diggers

Published by Creative Education

P.O. Box 227, Mankato, Minnesota 56002

Creative Education is an imprint of The Creative Company

www.thecreativecompany.us

Design and production by Rob & Damia Design

Art direction by Rita Marshall

Printed in the United States of America

Photographs by Getty Images (Roger Viollet/Getty Images), iStockphoto
(Matt Atkins, Christine Balderas, Chris Hill, Mario Hornik, Maria Jeffs,
Danish Khan, Stanislav Komogorov, Jerry McElroy, Guillermo Perales,
Robert Pernell, Kriss Russell, Sreedhar Yedlapati)

Library of Congress Cataloging-in-Publication Data

Gilbert, Sara.

Diggers / by Sara Gilbert.

p. cm. — (Machines that build)

Includes index.

ISBN 978-1-58341-728-7

1. Excavating machinery—Juvenile literature. I. Title. II. Series.

TA735.G555 2009

629.225—dc22   2007051662

First edition

9 8 7 6 5 4 3 2 1

CREATIVE EDUCATION

Diggers

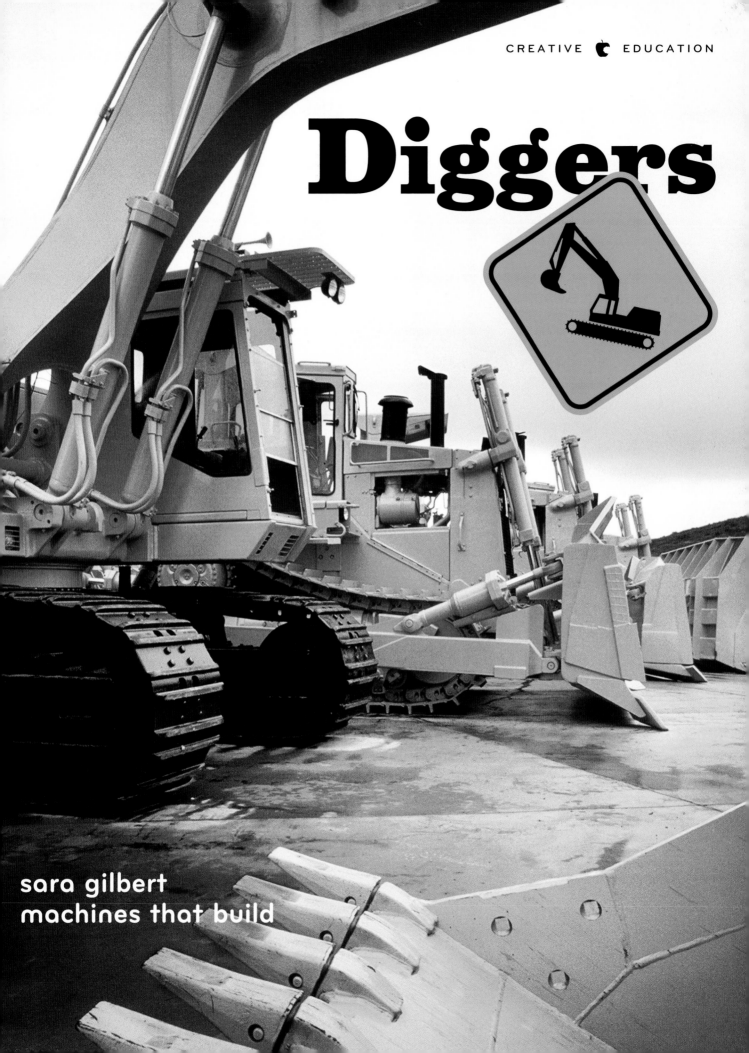

sara gilbert
machines that build

A digger is a big machine. Diggers make big holes in the ground. They have important jobs at construction (*con-STRUK-shun*) sites.

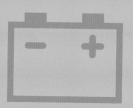

Diggers work in the dirt and mud all day long.

*A digger piles up the dirt
when it digs a ditch.*

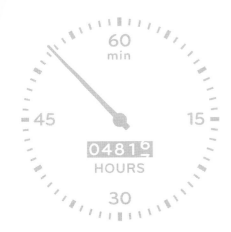

Diggers are used to make holes for new buildings to be built. They dig stone and rock out of *quarries* and mines. They dig ditches. They even dig mud out of the bottom of rivers.

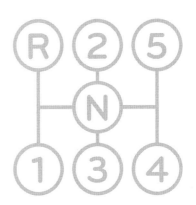

The bucket can have a smooth or toothed edge.

Most diggers have a long arm with a giant bucket.

EXCAVATOR PATTERN

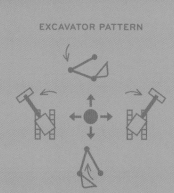

The bucket scoops up dirt.

In one scoop, some diggers can lift 6,000 pounds (2.7 t) of dirt!

*The belts of crawler tracks
are often caked with dirt.*

An operator sitting in a cab

Diggers move on big wheels or on wide, *steel* belts called crawler tracks. Crawler tracks help diggers move over bumpy ground. Some diggers have *cabs* that can turn around. Then the *operator* can see in every direction.

The first diggers were used in the United States in the 1830s. They were big shovels built on to train cars. Miners used the diggers to get *coal* out of mines.

Diggers in the 1920s did not have closed-in cabs.

Different diggers work on different projects. Excavators (*EX-kuh-vay-terz*) are used to make space for large buildings and to dig ditches. Backhoes and front-end loaders work on roads and smaller buildings. Mini diggers work in yards and tight spaces.

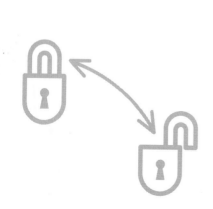

Diggers can be large or small
and work in many places.

A backhoe's two arms can do different jobs.

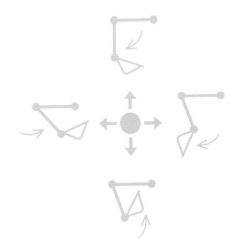

Backhoes have two arms. One arm is in the front, and the other arm is in the back. Each arm uses a different tool to do a different job. The operator's seat can turn around to face either direction.

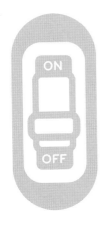

R ← Ⓝ → F

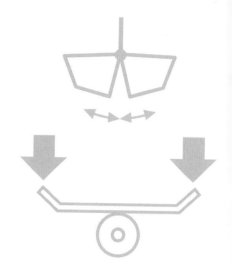

A digger reaches down to the ground with its arm. It scoops up a load of dirt with its bucket. Then it raises its arm and spins around. The dirt is dropped into a dump truck or onto a big pile.

A digger has to dump its full load after each scoop.

Joysticks can be moved in many directions.

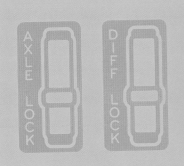

Digger operators use *joysticks* to move the arms up and down. Joysticks also control the bucket. The operator uses a joystick to tilt the bucket and dump the load. Then the operator is ready to dig down and scoop up another load!

Activity: Be a Digger

Find a spoon, a small bowl, or a toy shovel to use as a scoop. Try digging a hole in a sandbox or garden with each one (but be sure to check with an adult before you start). Which one can scoop the most dirt or sand? Which one would you want to have on a digging machine?

Glossary

cabs: the places where machine operators sit

coal: a black rock found underground that is used for fuel

joysticks: controllers that move up and down and from side to side

operator: the person who controls a machine

quarries: big, deep holes in the earth where people dig for stone

steel: a strong material that is hard to break

Read More About It

Llewellyn, Claire. *Mighty Machines: Truck.* New York: DK Publishing, 2000.

Richards, Jon. *Diggers and Other Construction Machines.* Brookfield, Conn.: Millbrook Press, 1999.

Index

24